Wordpress

The Ultimate Beginners Guide: A step by step guide to create your first website or blog without any programming or design knowledge

Table Of Contents

Introduction

Thanks to WordPress, publishing a website has never been this easy. Unlike before, ordinary internet users can now create websites with little knowledge about HTML or any scripting language. What is WordPress anyway?

WordPress is a Content Management System or CMS program built in PHP. CMSs are web applications that, as the name suggests, manage website content such as blog posts, images, and even videos. To make it simple, it is like a big website template that has been premade, for you not to bother creating or writing lines of code. All you need to do are to customize it with the help of intuitive graphical interfaces and tools then input the content that you want to display on your website.

If WordPress is just one of the many CMSs out there in the web, why choose WordPress instead of the other CMSs? Well, few of the biggest factors why many people prefer WordPress are simplicity, wide array of customization, popularity, and the community.

The simplicity of WordPress is ideal for those who have little idea on how the web works and have little knowledge when it comes to web development. With its user friendliness, almost everybody can master using WordPress in no time.

However, it does not mean that WordPress is only ideal for beginners. WordPress has advanced features and customizations that even most veteran web developers would appreciate. Not to mention that creating WordPress sites for them is like a walk in the park. With advanced knowledge in CSS, HTML, and WordPress template tags, they can transform an ordinary looking WordPress blog into one of the most complex websites on the web. And they can do that without spending too much time changing the internal workings of WordPress or developing additional client or server side scripts to manage the content they want to display.

Popularity and the community are additional bonuses that most WordPress users appreciate. With a large community, bugs and issues can be collected immediately and be fixed as fast as the developers can. On the other hand, the same community acts as WordPress' primary support group. If you got trouble or something you want to know, you can just go to WordPress' forums and ask it. Within minutes (or days in some occasion), you will get an answer right away.

On the other hand, with many developers indulging themselves with WordPress, the number of plugins and themes available on the market steadily increases. Due to that, WordPress can be customized in more ways than one. Also, the plugins make it possible for users to get the functionalities they want fast without, of course, developing by their own. All they need to do is go the plugins section of their dashboard, search for a plugin, and install it. Within minutes, the plugin will be live and working.

If you were convinced to get WordPress and use it for your website, then this book is for you. It contains basic as well as some advanced topics on how you can take full advantage of WordPress.

If you would like to get a free bonus chapter on how to make money with your first website or blog then you should subscribe to our mailing list:

http://eepurl.com/5N1z5

This is 100% free and we will also keep you up to date of our newest book releases.

Chapter 1: How to Install WordPress in a Few Mouse Clicks

Installing WordPress in your website is not that difficult to do. Whether you are going to use an installation wizard like Softaculous or Fantastico or a web host manager program, WordPress installation only requires you to click a few buttons and fill up a few forms.

However, even though it is that simple, you will need to be familiar with a few things. First, you should check if your computer or web host is capable of running WordPress. Second, you should know how to navigate your web directory or use an FTP client. Lastly, a bit of familiarity with your site's database is needed, too.

In case your web host does not have a WordPress or CMS installation wizard, you will need to download the installer and upload it to your web host or server.

To get the latest WordPress installer, go to http://wordpress.org/download/. The installer is not that large (it should be around 6 – 7 Mb), so it will not take a long time before you get it.

After getting the installer, you must upload it and extract it in your web host. Most directory explorers in webhost management applications has a command for that, so you will not need to do anything special in order to unzip the file on your web host. Alternatively, you can do it with ease with an FTP client.

On the other hand, some web hosts do not allow extraction. If that is the case, you will need to extract the installation file in your computer first, and then upload it to your website. If you are going to go this route, you will certainly need an FTP client since the content of the WordPress installation package contains hundreds of files and folders. And manually uploading them one by one on your browser can be a pain.

By the way, before you extract the files, make sure that you extract and place the file on the location that you want your WordPress website to appear. If you want your WordPress site to appear when your domain name is accessed, then you must place and extract the installation file in the root directory (public_html, htdocs, or httpdocs). Consult your web host provider if you do not know where your root directory is. On the other hand, if you want to install it in a subdirectory, you will need to create a folder and place the installer there.

For example, if you want to place your WordPress blog on www.examplesite.com/blog/, then create a folder named blog on your root directory.

Database

Once you have extracted the contents of the zip installation file, then it is time to create a database for your WordPress website. A database is a storage location where your WordPress installation will keep most of its files and contents. Meaning, all the changes and posts that you will place in your website will be saved there. Without it, your installation will not work.

Unfortunately, there are multiple tools that you might encounter for you to create a database. Nevertheless, for a WordPress installation, just making one will not involve complicated processes. Usually, many database tools in your web host are easy to understand. Also, you can get help from the web host's customer support department.

Anyway, creating a database is simple. All you need to is to create a name for your database. After that, add a user in your database.

When you are going to add a user, you will need to create a username and password for that user for it to be able to access the database you created. Take note, this username and password will not be the same username and password that you will use to access your WordPress website later. It will be a username and password for the database, which WordPress will use in order to store and access data on your database.

By the way, make sure that you secure the username and password that you will create for your database. Hackers target databases in order to gain access to your important data and even manipulate the content of your site.

Then, make sure that you grant the user with all the privileges it can have. Without those privies, your WordPress installation will have limited access to your database.

Installing WordPress

After you establish your database, take a note of all the information you created. You will need to your WordPress installation later. Then it is time to access the installation page of WordPress. Its location should be wp-admin/install.php. If you placed the installation files on the root directory, you will need to access www.examplesite.com/wp-admin/install.php. Once you do that, you will do the famous 5-minute WordPress installation.

Creating Configuration File

Actually, you are going to skip a step. Normally, you will need to configure your WordPress' wp-config file. However, it is a tad complicated to do. And one mistake may cost you to repeat the process. By accessing the install page, you can do it with the help of a user interface, so it will be a lot easier.

In the first step, you will be required to configure the wp-config file before you proceed. Press the Create a Configuration File button. You will be then redirected to a page where explanations on the next steps that you will do can be found. If you are finished reading all the explanations, click on the Let's Go button on the bottom of the page.

Database Setup

After that, you will be redirected to the database setup page. You will need to indicate the name of the database where you want WordPress to save its settings and content. Also, provide the username and password you created for that database. If you do not, or if you provided the wrong information, your WordPress will not be able to access the database and your installation will not progress.

Next will be the database host. By default, it will be set to localhost. It is best to leave it untouched if you are installing your WordPress at the same web host where your database was established. On the other hand, you can just bypass the table prefix text box. However, in case you are going to do multiple installs of WordPress in your site or the site already has an installation, you need to change its database for your current installation to avoid conflicting with the old or future WordPress installation.

Once you complete all the information needed on that page, click on the Submit button.

Setting Up WordPress

After the database is connected to WordPress, it is time to configure some of the basic setup for your website. In the new page, you will name your website, create your username and password for your WordPress site, and email address.

By the way, the last part of the page will ask you if you want to keep your website private – meaning search engines will not try to index or place your website in search engine results. Of course, place this check if you want your site to gain presence on the internet. However, you can leave it unchecked if you do not want search engines to index your website immediately. You can change this option later in case you think your site already has enough content and is ready to be indexed.

Checking Your New Site

After that, press the Install WordPress button. Just wait a few seconds (or minutes in some cases), and your WordPress should be ready. It was not that hard and long, right? Once it displays success page, you can already go ahead and access your site. By that time, it will contain some default content. On the other hand, you can also go ahead and access your dashboard by going to the wp-admin page. If you have installed your WordPress on your root directory, it should be accessible by going to www.examplesite.com/wp-admin/.

On that page, it will ask for your username and password for WordPress. And notice that on the same page, you can request for a password reset in case you forget your password. When that happens, the reset will be sent to the email that you indicated in the installation.

Anyway, if you log in to that page, you will be transferred to your website's dashboard. Remember, that dashboard is only meant to configure your WordPress website. You cannot manage your web host account there, your databases, or files in the server. Take your time to explore that page, to learn more about the things you can do with your WordPress installation.

Chapter 2: How to Publish Posts

You've already looked at your website and your WordPress dashboard. Now, you might be already interested on seeing your own post in your website. Thankfully, it is easy to create one.

In your dashboard, look for the Posts option on the sidebar on the left of your screen. It should be between Store and Media. In some older versions, it should be between Dashboard and Media. Click on the Posts option. Once you do that, the dashboard will refresh, the Posts option will expand, and the Posts page will be on the screen.

In this page, all the recent posts that you have published will be shown. If you want to add a post, just click on the Add New button besides the Posts header on top of the page. Alternatively, you can click on the Add New option below the Posts option on the sidebar.

Default Post Editor

You will be taken the Add New Post page. In the middle, there will be a simple text editor with a few formatting buttons on top. The formatting buttons can allow you to bold, italicize, and strike through text. Also, you can change the alignment on your text (align left, center, and align right) and create bullets and numberings for your lists.

Aside from the basic formatting buttons that will be shown to you by default, you can access some more text formatting options by pressing the toolbar toggle button. Once you do that, you can assign predefined text styles, underline, justify, change the font color, and indent your text on your posts.

And as a bonus feature, the text editor of WordPress comes with a basic proofreading tool from After the Deadline. It can detect simple style and spelling errors. It would help you a lot, especially if you have no access to word processors with good grammar and proofreading tools like Microsoft Word. On the other hand, just above those formatting buttons are some extra buttons that can let you add media (pictures or videos), a poll, a contact form, and location.

In case you want more control on the appearance of your post and you're a bit knowledgeable about HTML, you can change the default visual view of the text editor to text view. The text view will allow you to see the raw HTML form of the post you are going to publish. In case you want to insert some other HTML elements that the visual view do not provide on its formatting toolbar, you can simply add them via HTML code in text view.

Just on top of everything will be the title text box. You can indicate any title that you want in your post. The title will be automatically displayed as a header by the way. Once you type something on the title text box, WordPress will immediately create a permalink (or URL) for your post. It will be based on your post's title and the permalink settings that you might have changed on the settings of your WordPress site.

In case you do not like the auto-generated permalink, you can edit it. Near the generated permalink, there should be an edit button. Just click it, and you will be able to change the permalink.

On the right hand of the screen, some post options can be toggled. A few of them are the draft, preview, status, move to trash, and publish button. Just below those options, the format section is located. Depending on your post, you can just pick the right type on that place and your post will be formatted automatically. For example, if you want to show many pictures, it is best that you choose the gallery formatting option.

Just below the formatting section is the categories and tags section. You might already have an idea what those two sections are for; nevertheless, for the sake of those who do not know, you can sort your posts into categories and put tags on your posts to be able to further categorize them. It also helps when it comes to site navigation, too. For example, if a user wants to see all your posts about a certain topic, they can just click on a category or tag for your WordPress site to filter all the posts that are included on that topic.

New Text Editor

On your Add New post page, there should be a small notification bar there that would inform you that you should try WordPress' new post editor. A link to that new editor should be there. The new editor has a larger workspace; however, you will be out of your dashboard. In case that you only plan to post, using this editor will be a much better choice since it is less cluttered and compact.

After you finish writing your post, you can just click on the publish button on the text editor page. It will appear instantly on your website. By the way, in case you want to delay its publish time or set a date for the post to appear, you can edit it using the edit link beside the publish immediately section. A date and time form will appear, and in there, you can specify the date and time when the post will appear.

On the other hand, if you think your post is not ready yet to be published or you need to stop writing and you want to save the post for later editing, you can just click the save draft button. After that, you can just close the page and revisit the Posts page to open the draft post once more. By the way, WordPress automatically saves your draft every few minutes, so you can be a bit confident that you will not lose your work when your computer suddenly shuts down or if your browser closes unexpectedly.

Chapter 3: How to Give Your Website a Professional Touch

To match up with the appearance of most websites today, you will need to give your WordPress site with a bit of professional touch. How? By adding pictures and videos. The days of text only websites are already gone. And visitors always expect some eye candy whenever they browse websites.

Thankfully, WordPress allows you to include videos or photos in your posts with ease. By just clicking on Add Media on the Add New Post page, you can just upload or reinsert an old image or video saved in your website.

Once you click the Add Media button, a popup window will be overlaid on your dashboard. In it, you can click on the Select Files button to upload the images or videos you want to be saved on your website. In case you are not fond of choosing your files inside a dialog box, you can just drag and drop the files you want. Easy, right?

By the way, the uploader or insert media function does not apply to videos and images alone. You can also upload and display PDFs, Word documents, Excel spreadsheets, and PowerPoint presentations.

To make sure that your files will be searchable in search engines, fill up the descriptions form on the right hand part of the window. Give them a relevant title and description. Also, you can place captions if you want. And never forget to put something on the alt text. If you do not, there is a high chance the search engines will improperly index your file.

Before you insert the image or video, you can format its appearance on the same window. You can change its alignment, linking behavior, and display size. On the other hand, you can perform some basic image editing process on WordPress. On the top right corner of the window, just beside the thumbnail, you will see a link that says Edit Image. Click on it. The editing processes you can perform are scaling, cropping, rotation, and flips. Once you are done, just click on Save. And if you think the image is ready for display, just click on the Insert into post button located on the bottom right corner of the window.

On the other hand, if you just want to reinsert a file that you already uploaded before, you can go to the Media Library tab. In there, you can choose the file you want, and click on the Insert into post button.

Image Files from Other Websites

In case that you do not have a file to upload, but you want to use a media file from another website, you can do it by going to the Insert from URL. You can access it by clicking its link located on the left part of the upload window. Just copy the location of the file you want to insert and paste it into the URL text box. WordPress will fetch the file, and you will be able to place a caption, put an alt text, change its alignment, and change its linking behavior on that same page.

By the way, before linking or getting images from other websites, make sure that you have gained permission to use the file. In case you do not want waste some time getting permissions, you can use royalty-free images from the internet. But even though they are royalty free, make sure that you credit the source of that file and follow any policies set by the source.

YouTube Videos

Also, you can post YouTube videos, too! You can do that by going to the Insert YouTube section. Its link should be above the Insert URL link. On the same page, you can search the video from YouTube that you want to insert. You can search by the video title or by searching a specific user. Once you find the video you want, click on it, and click on the Insert button on the bottom right corner of the page.

Chapter 4: How to Customize Your Web Design

WordPress has become a popular content management system because of its user friendliness. Designing and customizing a WordPress website does not require you to be a professional developer. Even if that is the case, even web publishing experts choose it. After all, this content management system's customizability can save a lot of their time, especially if they are building a website for a client that requested them to have it up and running as soon as possible.

On it dashboard, multiple tools and options are laid out for you to be able to customize the look, feel, and functionality of your website without changing any line of code. The easiest way to do all of that is by changing your website's theme.

The first place you must explore to get an idea on how to change the design of your website is the Appearance page on your dashboard. Just go there, and you will see a menu that will offer your multiple options on how you will change your site's design without needing to code anything.

Themes

The first option in the appearance page in your dashboard is Themes. In WordPress, you have the option to choose from thousands of themes made by hobbyists and professional web developers. Just downloading, installing, and using it will change a website in a snap. And it only requires a click of a button.

Fortunately, you do not need to waste a lot of time to find a good theme for your site. Most themes available from WordPress are categorized, and can be filtered according to theme color, design, post formats, etc. Also, if you want to know the most used, popular, and newest themes in WordPress, it will be displayed on the page. All you need is to browse around.

In case that you want to see what the theme offers, you can just hover on the sample thumbnail of the theme and click on the Details button that will appear (or you can just click on the thumbnail). A popup window will show a short description of the theme, a bigger picture of the sample front page of the theme, the name of the creator (together with a link of the creator's website), and the category tags of the theme.

Below the popup page, you will see buttons: Activate, Preview, and Demo. Pressing activate will be the same as downloading, installing, and activating the theme for your website. The Preview button, on the other hand, will redirect you to your home page with the theme temporarily applied to it. With it, you will immediately see if your website and its contents will fit with the theme perfectly.

Also, the preview page will have a customization bar on it for you to be able to change and edit the design of theme real time. You do not need to waste your time and download the theme before you see how much customization you can do in order to create the design that you want for your website. In addition, the preview page allows you to toggle different device views for your page. On the bottom of the page, there will be a small floating tool bar that has three buttons. The first button is the PC monitor view, the second is tablet view, and the third one is mobile device view.

And lastly, pressing the Demo button will redirect you to a sample website or blog that uses the theme. Also, some demo pages have links to other pages that use different theme templates. You can also view them for you to get a feel on its design and see if it suites your website. Usually, demo pages provide more information about the theme, including some tips on how you can customize it to your liking.

By the way, there are two types of themes that you can get from WordPress – Free and Premium. Thankfully, the free themes are readily accessible from the Theme page and you can even search for any theme that you like. Fortunately, most of them are designed well, and offers the standard looks and functionality of a regular website.

On the other hand, premium themes offer a lot more. Most premium themes come with additional functions and widgets. And they offer a lot more customizations than the regular free themes. Also, you will get support from the team that made the theme. In case that you have one customization that you want to apply but cannot do it on your own, you can just contact them and get help.

If you already have a theme active, you can customize it to your liking. Usually, the theme installed on your website will be placed first on the list on the Themes page (it will have the word Active besides its name). Its thumbnail will have a Customize button. Click that if you want to change a few things in your website's design. The link will transfer you a preview page where you can edit the looks of your theme and site. Alternatively, you can access the customization page on the Appearance menu. Its link location should be just below the Theme button.

In case that you choose a premium theme, all of its customization will be active. On the other hand, take note that some free themes offer lesser customization options while some will allow you to have access to more customization options if you buy their premium versions.

One of the most common customization options offered by themes are background image or color change together with theme palette color change. On the other hand, the customization can allow you to change the site's title, header, your front page's display behavior, and widgets placement.

Widgets

By default, WordPress has multiple widgets that you can place on your site. Widgets are small snippets of code that provide certain functionalities for your website. A few common widgets that you might have seen before are the recent posts, recent comments, and meta widgets.

Commonly, widgets are placed on side columns or bars. Some are placed on footers – depending on the theme that you will use for your WordPress website. Fortunately, adding widgets is not that hard. All you need to do is go to the Widgets page on your dashboard, which is located in the Appearance menu. Choose the widgets you want to appear on your site by dragging and dropping the widget's title on the widgets columns or location that you will find on the rightmost part of the page. Do not worry if you think that you are not familiar with these widgets. The list of widgets comes with brief descriptions that you will surely understand when you read them. By the way, you can place multiple instances of the same widget on your website.

After getting the widgets you want to appear, you can rearrange the order on how they will appear on the website. You can change the title of the widgets to any name that you want. You can also edit some minor settings by expanding the widget's button. For example, you can limit the number of recent of blog posts to appear on the widget by fiddling on its settings. And in that same setting page, you can delete the widget you do not need anymore on your page. Do not worry; it will not disappear on your widgets list. It will just be removed from your page.

Plugins

After you install your WordPress website and try fiddling with it for a few days, you can start adding additional features to it by installing plugins. Plugins are small snippets of code that provide additional functionality to your website. Downloading one might provide you extra widgets, extra customization options on your dashboard, or extra menus on your website.

You can easily download these plugins from the plugins page in your dashboard. And just like themes, you can just search for the widget you want and install it in one click. By the way, there are free and premium plugins, too. However, be reminded that unlike themes, some plugins might be incompatible with certain WordPress versions while some are poorly programmed and might even make your site crash. Due to that, it is recommendable for you to steer clear of most free plugins, except those that have been rated and reviewed as safe and functional.

By the way, this section is not applicable for those users that have sites in WordPress.com. Unfortunately, they do not have the option to use and install plugins on their sites. For you to be able to use plugins, your site or WordPress must be hosted in your computer or a web host.

On the other hand, searching and installing plugins using the plugin search function of WordPress is not the only way to install plugins. You can also manually upload any plugins that you have by going to the upload tab or section in the plugin page in your WordPress dashboard.

Alternatively, if you are fond of using FTP clients, you can upload the plugin that you want to install using your FTP client. Take note, when uploading plugins; make sure that you do not upload them in zip form. Just copy or upload the file of the plugin on the plugins folder in your WordPress installation.

Fortunately, WordPress will do all the work after that. Once you visit the Plugins page in your dashboard, WordPress will automatically detect the plugin that you have uploaded. In there, you can activate it for you or your WordPress site to use it.

Chapter 5: Advance WordPress Themes Customization – An Overview

As the chapter's name implies, this section will talk about advanced methods on customizing your WordPress website's theme. Take note the things you will learn here is what will set your website apart from other websites. Even if you are using the same theme as they are using, yours will be unique once you apply what you will learn here.

First of all, this part will require you to have basic knowledge of PHP, HTML, and CSS. If you are not familiar with those two, then you can skip this chapter, and just get back here once you reach the end of the book. After all, you will still get the idea once you read this chapter. It is just that you will not be able to implement it right away.

Anyway, the regular theme customization in WordPress is very limited and basic. After all, you have already seen a lot of websites before, and you might have seen the difference between your site and theirs. In case that you want to join their league, then you need to customize your theme to the core.

Styles

Every element in your WordPress page is styled by a single stylesheet. And fortunately, you can edit that stylesheet anytime that you want. For you to access the stylesheet, go to your dashboard, click on appearance, and click on editor. On that page, you will be able to edit almost all WordPress core files, which include the stylesheet.

To edit the stylesheet, go to the bottom part of that page and click on the Stylesheet or style.css. Once you do, the page will refresh, and the edit text box will display the content of the style.css of your theme.

In there, you can edit all the styles set by your theme. However, make sure that you know how to edit and how the CSS syntax works. Also, it is not advisable to edit everything included on that file, especially the comments on the top most part. That comment section actually links that stylesheet to your theme. In addition, it is advisable for you to leave the CSS reset part on the beginning of the file alone.

The Loop

The Loop is a WordPress process that parses and displays the contents or posts of your website. It is called the Loop because the process will loop until all conditions have been satisfied. One of the conditions is the max number of posts it has to display.

For example, if the max number of post your site is set to five, then the loop will check your database for posts that match its criteria. It will not stop until it gets five posts or until it reaches the end of the database.

The code for the Loop is located at the main index template or index.php. Technically, it is your website's homepage. Take note that recklessly editing this file can result into unexpected display errors on your homepage. Always create a backup for this file.

It will be best to try to take a sneak peek on your index.php file for you to get familiarized with the loop. As you can see, the code inside the file is mostly written in PHP. In the first part of the code, the main page's header is called out. Then after that, the conditions for the Loop appear.

Usually, the condition for the loop requires the page to check the maximum number of posts that will be displayed. Also, it will check if your database has enough posts. As it skims through the content that you have saved, it will count how many posts it has displayed.

After the declaration of conditions, you will see the post template. If you are familiar with HTML, CSS, and PHP, you might have seen a few elements that are unfamiliar to you. They are mostly WordPress Template Tags. Declaring a template tag on the index file will make the server return a value. For example, if you place title(); on the file, the server will return and display the title of the post being parsed by the Loop.

Well, this section will not go any further than that.

Child Themes

Another method to change your WordPress site's theme is to take advantage of child themes. Child theme is a pseudo theme that is commonly created in order to prevent the user from changing any part of the file of the theme that he is using.

Also, child themes are used to make sure that the changes that you will create in your themes will be retained whenever the main theme you are using gets updated. Remember that whenever the theme gets updated, any changes you made in it will be overwritten by the new version. Due to that, it is best practice to use child themes whenever you want to go deep in customizing your theme.

To create a child theme, use your FTP client and go to the themes folder of your WordPress installation. Duplicate the theme's folder and files in the themes folder that you want to have a child with. Rename the duplicate theme's folder with the same name of the original theme and attach a '-child' without single quotes on the end of its name. It is not really necessary, but it is a standard practice.

After that, go to the duplicate's style.css and edit its headers. If you are going to create a child for the Twenty Fourteen theme, here are the changes that you must do:

```
/*
 Theme Name:    Twenty Fourteen Child
 Theme URI:     http://example.com/twenty-fourteen-child/
 Description:   Twenty Fourteen Child Theme
 Author:        John Doe
 Author URI:    http://example.com
 Template:      twentyfourteen
 Version:       1.0.0
 Tags:          light, dark, two-columns, right-sidebar, responsive-layout, accessibility-ready
 Text Domain:   twenty-fourteen-child
*/
```

Once you have done that, you can now use the child theme. Go to your dashboard and go to the Themes page. If you did not mess up changing the values on the head of your child theme's style.css, the child theme will appear on your themes list. You can now activate it, and create a modification on the style without worrying about it being overwritten by updates.

Chapter 6: How to use Search Engine Optimization to get ranked better by Google

To get your website more noticed by the world, you need to apply search engine optimization to your site. Search engine optimization is a set of web or content development techniques that aim to make a website or web page more "friendly" to search engines – primarily to Google. Being friendly to search engines means that your site must be set to be get noticed by search engines and be posted more often or in higher places in search page results.

Thankfully, WordPress has already integrated SEO on its system. Even if you do not actually perform SEO, you can rest assured that search engines will notice your website, especially if you are posting high quality content.

However, you can still amplify your SEO value by doing some tweaks on your website.

Whenever you post pictures on your site, make sure to never forget to indicate a title, alt text, and description for it. Nowadays, image search has become a powerful tool to lure in more potential visitors.

Learn how to take advantage of headings in your posts. Headings provide points to your page or website's SEO value. With good title and headings, your relevancy to your target keyword goes up a notch.

Also, learn a bit of HTML and schematic markups. Schematic markups can make your links on the search results page richer. Each schematic you apply on your page will create additional links, snippets, or breadcrumbs on your website, which will allow for easier navigation. By the way, you need to learn HTML since schematic markups are written using HTML.

Take advantage of social media. Make sure that you connect your website to your social accounts in Facebook, Twitter, and Pinterest.

Also, connect your website to Google Webmaster and Bing Webmaster tools. Those websites or online tools can help you more with SEO. Become more familiar with them.

Always provide quality content. All those SEO tricks will be meaningless if you do not have high quality content. After all, that is what search engines advocate, especially Google.

Make sure that you proofread the articles you post. And make sure that your keywords are relevant to your topic.

Placing internal links on your website is a good idea to raise your SEO score.

Download some plugins that can enhance your SEO value. Many of them can be easily downloaded for free in WordPress. And just like before, always be careful whenever you are installing plugins. Some of them are untrustworthy and might result into trouble in the future.

Chapter 7: How to Choose a Great Domain Name

When choosing a great domain name, SEO must be applied. The first rule of thumb is to take advantage of same exact domain match or EMD. In layman's terms, the title or domain name of website must match the keywords you are targeting.

For example, if you are going to create a website that will focus on selling cars in California, using a domain name or website address such as www.buycarsfromcalifornia.com will be favorable for you.

Downside to Exact Match Domain

The downside when it comes to EMD is that most of the common business website names are taken, being used, or are parked. By the way, a parked domain name is an address that has been bought by user but he is not using it. Instead, he will wait for somebody who actually needs the address and sell it for a high price. You are actually lucky if somebody parked the domain name you desired since instead of waiting for someone to let go of it, all you need to do is buy it instead. Also, unlike before, search engines have started to lower the value of websites with exact match domain.

About Long Domain Names

On the other hand, using exact match domains might make you use a long domain name. Long domain names are a no-no. Not only that they are hard to memorize, but also it will take a lot of time before your visitor types it out completely on their browsers. And the longer the domain name, the higher their chances to make a spelling error and prevent them from accessing your website.

Domain Name and Brand

Using a brand name or your company's name as your domain's name is the complete opposite of EMD. However, unlike EMD, your domain name will not help you the early search engine optimization boost you might want. Nevertheless, if you build a good reputation around your brand name, you will experience its long term benefits.

One of the best examples of using brand names in domain names is Facebook. Just imagine, who would have thought that Facebook is a social media site? At first, people might think what is Facebook? Is it a face with a book? It does not really make sense at first. However, as Facebook's reputation grew larger, those previous questions disappeared. Now, the tables have turned. When people see websites with the words face and book, they will think if the website is related to Facebook or if it related to social media.

On the other hand, brand names as domain names are catchier, more memorable, and they are shorter. They are also easy to remember and type unlike longwinded exact match domain names.

Domain Name Extensions

Also, be mindful when choosing the domain name extension (e.g., .com, .net, .org, etc.). When you are going to make a website for an organization, it would be wise to use .org. On the other hand, if you are going to establish a business online, you might think that .biz would be the best choice. But to be honest, it is better to use .com instead.

It is unfortunate that many people are not familiar with the .biz domain extension. So in case they would type in your website's address, they might not find it since they are inclined to think that your domain's extension is .com. And in case that there is a site with the same name as yours, but is using the .com extension, you will lose one potential visitor or customer to one of your possible competitors.

Domain Name Checker

To see if a domain name is available for you to claim, you can use a domain name checking tool on the internet. GoDaddy has one, and here is the link to their domain name checker tool: https://www.godaddy.com/domains/domain-name-search.aspx.

Just type in the domain you want to check on text box and press on the Search Domain button. In case that the domain you want to have is unavailable, GoDaddy will provide you with similar domain names that you can get. Aside from that, it will also display the price of the domain names for you to have an idea if they will fit into your budget.

To secure the domain name that you want, you must immediately register it. However, do not be careless when it comes to domain registrations. Nowadays, many companies who claim to be reliable domain registrars are all over the web. Most of them only last for three months. They will just disappear – along with your domain name and money.

So, to prevent dealing with them, narrow down your choices. Below are few of the trustworthy and reliable domain registrars on the web:

- Domainsite
- Network Solutions
- GoDaddy
- Dotster

Reliable Web Hosting

Choosing the web host for your site will come as a challenge. Even though there are a lot of web host providers on the online world, you will be stuck with only a few options. Also, reliability is not only the main concern that you must consider. You must also choose a web host provider according to the pricing options they offer, extra features, and most importantly, customer support.

Anyway, below are the most recommended web host providers for WordPress users:

- InMotion Hosting: technical support has been this company's main selling point, which is ideal for complete newbies when it comes to web publishing. Aside from that, the servers of InMotion Hosting are very reliable. The company guarantees that its servers are always up 99.9% of the time.

- BlueHost: this has been one of the pioneers of web hosting services on the web. The company has started around the late nineties, and it is still going strong. For the last few years, it has maintained good reputation and a good ranking. Even WordPress developers recommend this site for first time WordPress users. One of its strong points is their stable servers. You will never worry about your site running slow.

- SiteGround: this company has been one of the most recognized alternate web hosts for the ones mentioned above. They focus on security, which will definitely make you not worry about your WordPress website being compromised. Also, the company offers their users with specific location hosting. As of now, they have three data centers that you can choose: Singapore, Europe, and USA.

- HostGator: if you want a simple and easy-to-manage web host account, then you can just choose HostGator. Its hosting plans are mainly geared towards WordPress users. It boasts its one-click WordPress installation. And the company's support team is capable and helpful.

- Web Hosting Hub: if you are going to use WordPress for your small business, then Web Hosting Hub will be your best choice. The company has very competitive pricing for their packages, and the accounts they provide are easy to manage thanks to their free website builder and control panel.

Chapter 8: How to Keep Your Website Secure

By default, a WordPress website is secure enough to prevent yourself from being attacked by malicious entities on the web. However, it does not mean it is immune to getting hacked.

The first thing to do is to find a server or web host that has multiple security features. Take note that those features will greatly add some additional cost. The second thing to do is to make sure that your WordPress installation is always up to date. The third thing to do is to secure your admin access to your WordPress site and your admin access to your web hosting account and website manager.

Also, take note that you, yourself, are a security risk. Whenever you are downloading themes and widgets, make sure that you are getting them from trustworthy sources. It is common that some poorly written or malicious plugins can easily create security loopholes in your website. You have been warned.

Free Scanning Tools

Also, you might want to regularly check if your website is compromised or hacked. You can do that by using a free remote scanner like the site check tool from Sucuri. The scan does not take a lot of time. And you will immediately see its results after you use it. A few of the things it will check are: if your site has malware, if your site is blacklisted, SPAM were injected on your site, and the status of your website's firewall.

Reporting WordPress Issues

On the other hand, in case that you think or find any possible security issues within WordPress, always make sure that you report it. Alternatively, if you find a plugin or theme that might be a potential security risk, you should also report it. For plugins, you can report it to WordPress by emailing them at plugins@wordpress.org. Also, as good practice, you must also contact the creator or developer about the problem with his or their plugin.

Preventive Measures Against Hacking

In case you feel that you have been hacked, you can perform an instant scan using two plugins. If you think you are dealing with an installed malware by a hacker, download and activate the plugin Anti-Malware and Brute-Force Security by ELI. On the other hand, if you think that someone is hacking your site by exploiting some of the loopholes in WordPress, you can use the plugin Exploit Scanner. The plugin will conduct a scan on your WordPress files and check if there were been any attempts of hacking on your website.

Virus and Malware

In some cases, some viruses and malware can attack your website through your computer. Due to that, it is also important that you keep your computer or host computer free from those malicious programs. Always keep your system updated and regularly scan it.

Getting Installation Files from WordPress.org

As a rule of thumb, never download or install WordPress installation packages from other websites beside from WordPress.org. Also, in case you have WordPress version 3.7 or higher, you will not to worry about manually updating your website since the auto update feature was already included in the latter versions of WordPress.

Take note that whenever an update gets released, it usually means that a security vulnerability is found, and the update is a patch that will fix it. Because of that, the possibility of your site being compromised gets high, so as good practice, always scan your site whenever an update becomes available. By the way, you will know if there is an update in your dashboard. You will be notified that your WordPress installation is out of date, and it will suggest an update.

On the other hand, if you want to use an old version of WordPress, use it your own risk since older versions of the program is more vulnerable to attacks.

Vulnerabilities of Your Web Host/Server

Of course, WordPress is not the only one with vulnerabilities. Your web host or server might have one or two, too. So you must be vigilant on what is happening on your host. Not only that, but you must also be informed on what kind of security measures and system your host is using for you to be able anticipate any possible attack. Take note that if you are part of a shared server, the possibility of your site being hacked is high if one of the websites in your shared group was hacked.

Data Backup

One of the ultimate precautions that you should perform regularly is backing up your data. Having an extra copy of your website files ensures you that whatever happens in your files or pages, you can just instantly rollback to a previous version of your site.

By the way, you might focus on creating backups of your files; however, the most essential part of your website that you should create a copy of is your database. Remember, all of your site's content will be saved in the database by WordPress. So, even if you have created a backup for your files, but you do not have a backup of your database, you will not be able to restore your site's content. Fortunately, most database management and webhost management systems have extra features that can provide you with automatic backups.

Reading Logs

Take your time to learn how to understand the content of your WordPress logs. Inside the logs, you will see every action done in your WordPress websites. In case that you feel that a certain user or visitor attempted to hack your website, you can track him down or be alerted by reading the logs of your WordPress website.

However, be reminded that the logs will not tell you exactly who did what. The logs only record IP addresses. Nevertheless, the IP and the time of the attack are already valuable information that can give you a heads up on the next move that you will make to protect your website.

Chapter 9: How to Solve the Most Common WordPress Problems

As mentioned before, WordPress is not exactly the perfect system. There will be glitches, errors, and security loopholes that may pop up from time to time.

However, it is unfortunate that most of the common WordPress problems are not generated by those things. Most of the problems actually come from user or admin mistakes. Due to that, this section will mostly about prevention on the most common WordPress problems.

Blank WordPress Screen

There can be multiple reasons that can result to a blank WordPress page. Before you panic when you see nothing but white screen on your website, troubleshoot first. Check to see if it is only happening on your end. It is common for browsers to display a white page if its connection to the internet is disrupted, so make sure that your internet connection is working fine.

Next is to try using another computer or internet connection. If it works on that other device or connection, then the problem's on your end. Alternatively, if it does not, then it is time to move to the next step.

Check if it is a server-related issue. Access your web host account, and see if your account is active and if you can access your files on the control panel of your website.

If the files are accessible, then it is time to do something about WordPress. There are three common reasons if the problem is isolated to WordPress.

First, WordPress might have tried to upgrade but failed. Again, that failure might have caused by an internet connection error (if you are running it on your computer or server) or server error if the website is on a webhost. To fix that, perform a manual patch. But unlike the next two, an auto upgrade error does not always result to a white screen. Your WordPress site will likely post an error message.

Anyway, the second reason is that you could have installed a faulty theme. And third, you might have installed a faulty or incompatible plugin.

To know whether it is a plugin or theme issue, disable all your plugins in your WordPress dashboard. If it still does not work, your theme might be causing the problem. If that's the case, create a backup of your theme if you heavily edited it – just to be on the safe side. After that, revert to the default WordPress theme Twenty Fourteen. That should be able to fix this issue.

On the other hand, if the theme is not the problem and disabling all your plugins solved the issue, start isolating the plugin that might have been causing the white screen. Do that by enabling your plugins one by one and refreshing your website.

In case that the theme that causing the problem is a premium theme, immediately contact the creator or support group for that theme for them to fix it or provide you with solutions. The same goes for the buggy plugin that might have caused this issue.

And that is the main reason why it pays to be careful in choosing your theme or plugins you will install. Most of the next issues that will be discussed here will always require you to check your themes or plugins for problems as the last troubleshooting steps.

Error Establishing a Database Connection

There are numerous possible causes of this error message. But in generally means that something is preventing your WordPress installation to access the database you have created.

One of the prime suspects that you must check is the wp-config file. You must make sure that the information regarding your database is correctly written there. The contents of wp-config can be a bit uneasy to the eyes. And take note that you must not change anything here unless you are sure that you know what you are doing. Mistakenly changing some of the settings here can make your WordPress website inaccessible. Anyway, below is the part of the wp-config file that you must check:

```
// ** MySQL settings - You can get this info from your
web host ** //
/** The name of the database for WordPress */
define( 'DB_NAME', 'database_name_here' );

/** MySQL database username */
define( 'DB_USER', 'username_here' );

/** MySQL database password */
define( 'DB_PASSWORD', 'password_here' );

/** MySQL hostname */
define( 'DB_HOST', 'localhost' );
```

You can use the text editor in your web host management system to open the file or you can just open it using your local text editor in your FTP client. As a good practice, make a duplicate of file before you change anything. And it is best to use your text editor's text function for you to immediately find the section mentioned above.

To make sure that the wp-config has no problems with accessing your database, make sure that the proper values are placed on the DB_NAME, DB_USER, DB_PASSWORD, and DB_HOST match the right values. As the values implied on their names, they are your database's name, the root account's username on your database, its password, and the address of your database respectively.

If you find out that those values were changed but you do not remember changing anything, it is possible that your website might have been hacked. Immediately perform some security scan on your WordPress installation by using the programs mentioned in the WordPress security chapter.

On the other hand, double check if your database is accessible through the database manager application in your web host. Make sure that the username and password that you have are working.

In case the database is inaccessible, it is possible that your server or your web host's database is currently down. This might happen if the database has reached its max number of access or bandwidth usage, or if the server itself is down. During these times, it is best for you to contact the customer support department of your web host provider.

Briefly Unavailable for Scheduled Maintenance – Check Back in a Minute

Usually, this is something you do not need to be frightened about. Whenever WordPress performs an auto update, it will automatically switch to maintenance mode. However, in case this error lasts for an hour, or even just 30 minutes, be alarmed.

It is possible that the auto update was not able to turn off the maintenance mode after WordPress updated. To fix it, log in to your web host management program or FTP client. Look for the .maintenance file. It should be on the root directory of your web host. Just delete it and the maintenance error will not appear anymore once you access your website. In case that the auto update failed, WordPress will attempt to upgrade again and the .maintenance file will reappear.

Website Not Updating Properly

Whenever the pictures you posts or the images you changed or edited does not update, your browser might be causing the problem. This usually happens if you perform small edits. This is a minor issue and it can be fixed by just clearing the cache of your browser.

Conclusion

Those are most of the things you need to learn about WordPress. If you are interested to learn more, it is advisable that you go to WordPress,org's Codex. Most of the advanced bits of info you need to learn about this CMS are located in there. However, be warned that the learning curve is a bit steep if you are not that well versed in web development. Still, if you're eager enough to learn, there's no reason to hesitate.

If you would like to get a free bonus chapter on how to make money with your first website or blog then you should subscribe to our mailing list:

http://eepurl.com/5N1z5

This is 100% free and we will also keep you up to date of our newest book releases.

Good luck in your web development career. Cheers!

www.ingramcontent.com/pod-product-compliance
Lightning Source LLC
Chambersburg PA
CBHW060937050326
40689CB00013B/3128